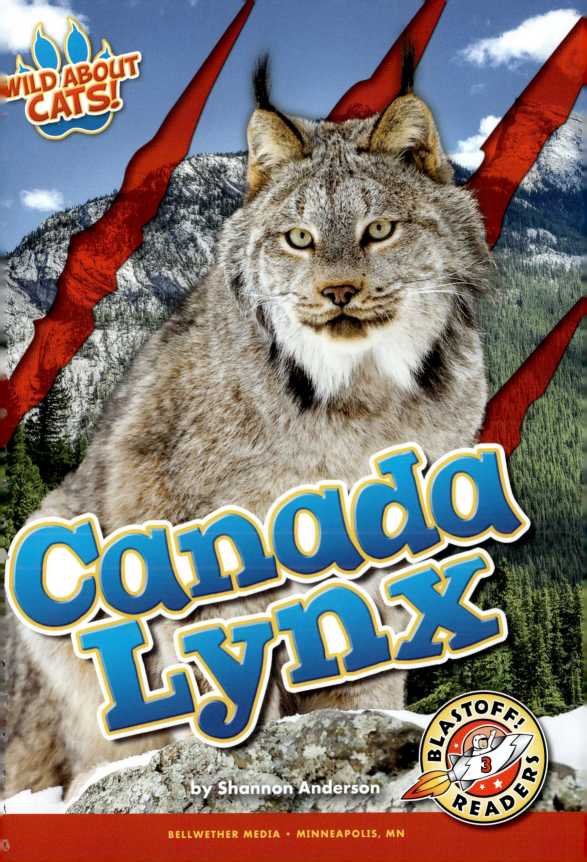

Blastoff! Readers are carefully developed by literacy experts to build reading stamina and move students toward fluency by combining standards-based content with developmentally appropriate text.

 Level 1 provides the most support through repetition of high-frequency words, light text, predictable sentence patterns, and strong visual support.

 Level 2 offers early readers a bit more challenge through varied sentences, increased text load, and text-supportive special features.

 Level 3 advances early-fluent readers toward fluency through increased text load, less reliance on photos, advancing concepts, longer sentences, and more complex special features.

★ **Blastoff! Universe**

Reading Level

 Grade K

 Grades 1–3

 Grade 4

This edition first published in 2025 by Bellwether Media, Inc.

No part of this publication may be reproduced in whole or in part without written permission of the publisher. For information regarding permission, write to Bellwether Media, Inc., Attention: Permissions Department, 6012 Blue Circle Drive, Minnetonka, MN 55343.

Library of Congress Cataloging-in-Publication Data

LC record for Canada Lynx available at: https://lccn.loc.gov/2024046818

Text copyright © 2025 by Bellwether Media, Inc. BLASTOFF! READERS and associated logos are trademarks and/or registered trademarks of Bellwether Media, Inc.

Editor: Suzane Nguyen   Designer: Brittany McIntosh

Printed in the United States of America, North Mankato, MN.

Table of Contents

Snow Walkers	4
Snow Cats	8
Hare Hunters	12
Lynx Litters	18
Glossary	22
To Learn More	23
Index	24

Snow Walkers

Canada lynx spend much of their time in snow. The toes on their paws spread. They walk on snow easier this way!

They live in **shrublands**, forests, and **grasslands**.

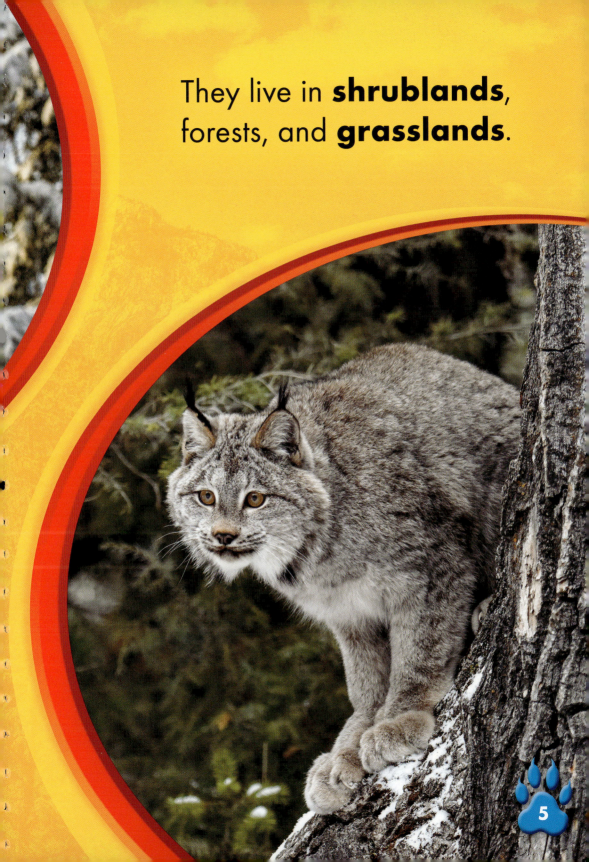

Canada lynx live across Canada. They are also found in Alaska.

Smaller numbers live in other parts of the United States. But **habitat** loss **threatens** them. People also harm these cats.

Snow Cats

These cats have reddish-brown fur. In winter, it turns light gray and grows thicker. Long back legs help the cats walk through deep snow.

The lynx have black fur on their tail tips and **ear tufts**.

Identify a Canada Lynx

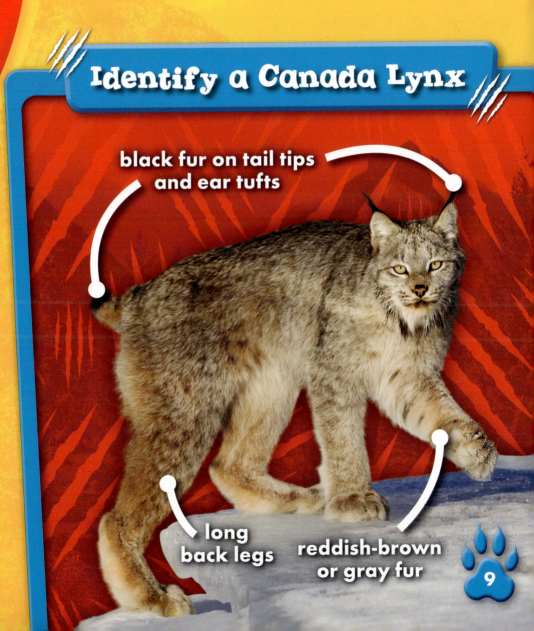

- black fur on tail tips and ear tufts
- long back legs
- reddish-brown or gray fur

9

Canada lynx are about 3 feet (0.9 meters) long. Their tails can grow up to 6 inches (15 centimeters) long.

Female lynx weigh around 19 pounds (9 kilograms). Males can weigh up to 38 pounds (17 kilograms).

Hare Hunters

Big eyes and great hearing help Canada lynx hunt at night.

Sometimes, the cats are **ambush** hunters. Other times, they **stalk** their **prey**. They follow closely, then the cats **pounce**!

Canada lynx are **carnivores**. They mostly eat snowshoe hares. The cats' numbers rise when there are more hares. Their numbers go down when there are fewer hares.

Canada lynx also eat grouse and squirrels.

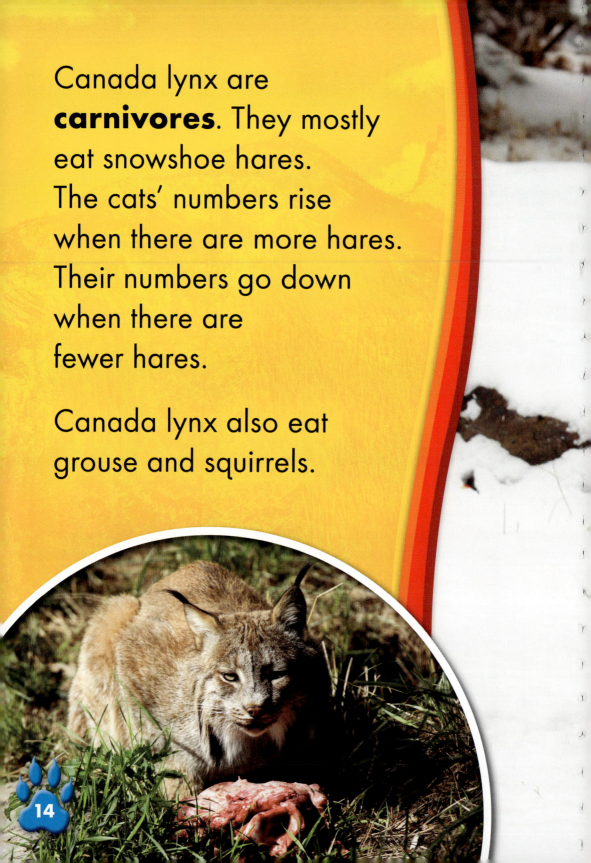

Canada lynx are **solitary**. But sometimes they live in small groups.

The cats are **crepuscular**. They are most active at dawn and dusk. They are awake at night, too.

Lynx Litters

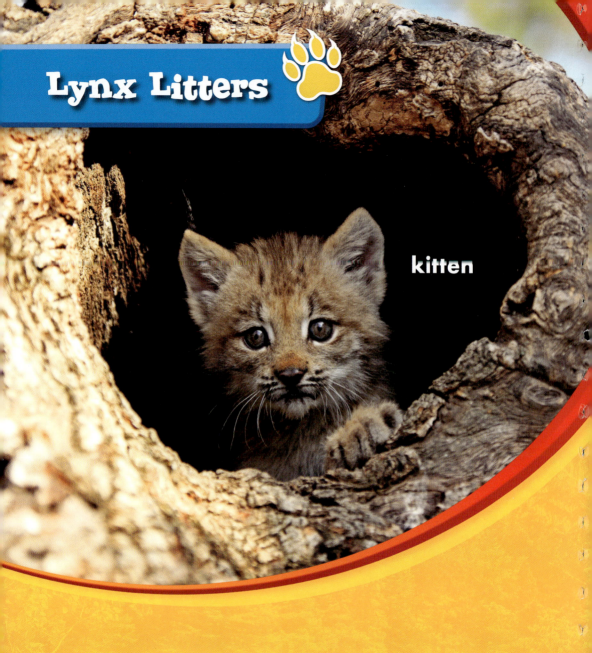

kitten

Female Canada lynx have **litters** of up to six kittens. The kittens stay in fallen logs or stumps to stay safe.

The mom raises the kittens on her own. She teaches them to hunt.

Baby Canada Lynx

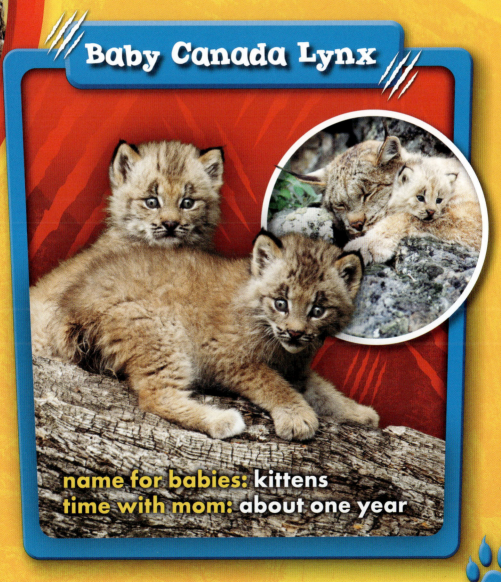

name for babies: **kittens**
time with mom: **about one year**

Kittens drink milk for about five months. Then they start eating meat. Kittens leave mom at about one year old.

Some kittens may stay together. Others leave on their own!

In the Wild

habitats:

shrublands   forests   grasslands

conservation status: least concern

Least Concern	Near Threatened	Vulnerable	Endangered	Critically Endangered	Extinct in the Wild	Extinct

population in the wild: unknown
population trend: stable in Canada and Alaska, going down in the rest of the United States
life span: up to 14 years in the wild

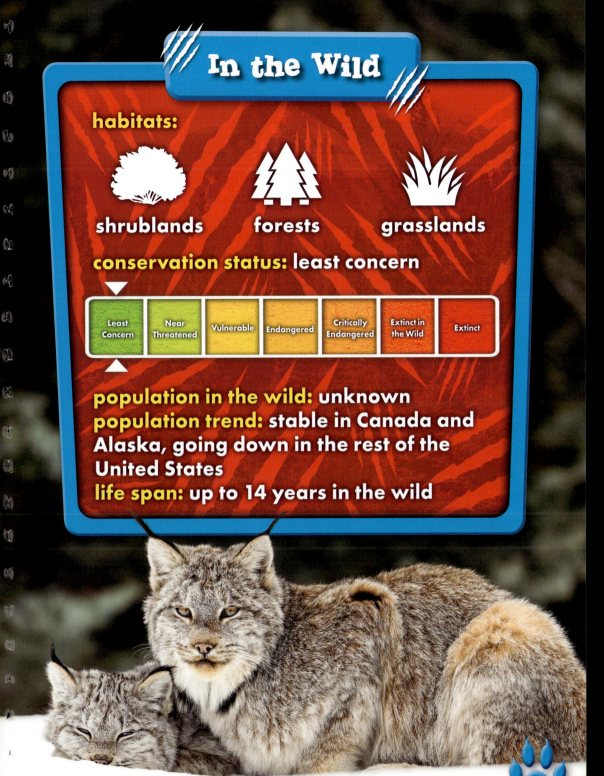

Glossary

ambush—related to an attack from a hiding place

carnivores—animals that only eat meat

crepuscular—most active during dawn or dusk

ear tufts—bunches of long hair on the tips of Canada lynx ears

grasslands—lands covered with grasses and other soft plants with few bushes or trees

habitat—the home or area where an animal prefers to live

litters—groups of babies that are born together at the same time

pounce—to suddenly jump on something

prey—animals that are hunted by other animals for food

shrublands—dry lands that have mostly low plants and few trees

solitary—living alone

stalk—to follow slowly and quietly

threatens—causes shrinking populations or increases the risk of dying out

To Learn More

AT THE LIBRARY

Geister-Jones, Sophie. *Lynx*. Mendota Heights, Minn.: Apex, 2022.

Jacobson, Bray. *Lynxes*. Buffalo, N.Y.: Gareth Stevens Publishing, 2024.

Schuh, Mari. *Bobcat or Lynx?* Minneapolis, Minn.: Bellwether Media, 2022.

ON THE WEB

FACTSURFER

Factsurfer.com gives you a safe, fun way to find more information.

1. Go to www.factsurfer.com.

2. Enter "Canada lynx" into the search box and click 🔍.

3. Select your book cover to see a list of related content.

Index

Alaska, 6
ambush, 13
Canada, 6
carnivores, 14
colors, 8, 9
crepuscular, 17
ear tufts, 9
eyes, 12
females, 11, 18, 19, 20
food, 14, 15, 20
forests, 5
fur, 8, 9
grasslands, 5
groups, 16
habitat loss, 7
hearing, 12
hunt, 12, 13, 19
identify, 9
in the wild, 21
kittens, 18, 19, 20
legs, 8
litters, 18
males, 11

night, 12, 17
numbers, 7, 14
paws, 4
pounce, 13
prey, 13, 14, 15
range, 6, 7
shrublands, 5
size, 10, 11
size comparison, 11
snow, 4, 8
solitary, 16
stalk, 13
tails, 9, 10
toes, 4
United States, 7

The images in this book are reproduced through the courtesy of: Dominique Braud/ Dembinsky Photo Associates/ Alamy, front cover (Canada lynx), p. 8; Levi Shultz, front cover (background); Chase D'animulls, p. 3; Gerald Corsi, p. 4; Evelyn D. Harrison, p. 5; Warren Metcalf, p. 6; Jukka Jantunen, pp. 9, 23; Jillian Cooper, pp. 10-11; Nynke van Holten, p. 11 (house cat); MikeLane45, p. 11 (Canada lynx); Keith Crowley/ Alamy, p. 12; wesdotphotography/ Alamy, p. 13; wrangel, p. 14; imageBROKER.com GmbH & Co. KG/ Alamy, pp. 14-15, 16, 18; FotoRequest, p. 15 (snowshoe hares); Jim Cumming, p. 15 (ruffed grouse); Robert Harding Video, p. 15 (red squirrels); robertharding/ Alamy, p. 17; Design Pics Inc/ Alamy, p. 19 (left); W. Perry Conway/ Getty Images, p. 19 (right); Dee Carpenter Originals, p. 20; Colleen Gara, pp. 20-21.